SLOW BURNING FIRES

To the next generation

'Look at all this beauty'
FLEUR ADCOCK,
Stewart Island

Slow Burning Fires

poems by

Diana Brodie

Paekakariki Press

2020

This is number 115
from an edition of 250 copies

Text © 2020, Diana Brodie
Images © 2020, Lily Witchell

ISBN: 978 1908133 42 7

Typeset in Monotype Garamond 156
and hand printed at Paekakarki Press,
Walthamstow.

Contents

Oranges from Matisse	1
Rainy Afternoon	3
Life in the Stone	4
Grandpa Joe	5
Looking for a Grandmother	6
This Place	7
The Last Day it Snowed	8
Back to the Room	8
Child and the Star Book	9
Uncle from Rome	10
Speaking of Mountains: The Land of the Long White Cloud	11
Woodsmoke	12
At the Turning	13
Moving on Ice	14
Dark Awakenings	15
Entering the Frame	16
Sleeping in a Strange Room	17
Firstborn	18
Word Attack	19
Bringing Back Birdman	20
Ravenous	21
Mollusc Child	22
The Fallen	23
Hanging on the Hickory	24
Acorn People	25
A Shadow of Myself	26

Oranges from Matisse

Matisse sent Picasso a box of oranges once a year. Picasso never ate them, but had them on display—as Matisse's oranges, only to be looked at.
Review of Matisse-Picasso exhibition
Guardian (7.5.02)

Two artists, one of them said, *as different
as the North Pole from the South.*
Argument. Derision. Rivalry.
But these oranges.
In the act of giving, anything can happen.

For Henri, an orange was merely that, an orange,
or oysters simply oysters; he loved things
for their colour and their texture, for themselves.
Observe his painting where, backlit by sunstreams
filtering through diamonds of a leaded window,
(purple curtains hanging limply to one side),
there's a square red table in the corner of a room.
Tight bunches of crimson and yellow flowers pattern
the loosely-folded tablecloth, and in the centre
there's an oval basket piled with tumbling lemons
and oranges, their dark glossy leaves still intact.

Pablo (on the other hand), master of cubism,
as of many things, saw a violin, a lover's face,
or an orange, from each intriguing aspect. He
broke up form, angled edges, overlapped
or interlocked their planes. Gave energy.

Included: the orange's remembered roundness,
the roughness of stroked peel felt in the fingertips.
Present: each shadow on its surface, every lightfall.
There too its history, the sights and smells
of Tangiers markets. The orange seen
as symbol—sun, perhaps, or breast or sphere,
accompaniment to the skull which looms
against the right-hand frame. At La Californie,
an open crate of oranges sits near the doorway.
A whitening, furry pelt spreads over the softening skin,
patches of green mould ooze like tears
washing the cheeks in Picasso's portrait
of the crying Dora.

What is an orange?
Though seen from all angles,
the truth is still not known.

Rainy Afternoon

Childhood was a long wet afternoon
listening to rain pebbles
    clanging on a tin roof.

When the rain skidded to a stop
against overflowing gutters,
    the voices would begin.

Don't go out, don't stare at the sun
    for fear of blindness.

So I lie still in a narrow room,
feet propped up against the wall,
    long before dark, listening

to the plop of ball against bat,
children fighting, playing
    in the dangerous streets.

Life in the Stone

Cool as a chapel, the letterer's workshop.
Laborare est orare. I'm left alone.
Through the half-open door from the garden
floats the pale, September light, faint
with birdsong. Stacked in the stoneyard
the lumps of greenish slate, boulders
wrenched from riverbeds, rolled down
Scottish hillsides. The craftsman
knows their histories and their poetry.

His chisels rest now on the workbench,
ritual objects connecting eye with mind
with hand. Propped against the wall
lie carved and finished stones, pulsing,
waiting for transport to chosen places.
Covering, sanctifying everything,
a silver ash of stone dust. I turn the pages
of the pattern books, with my finger trace
the letterforms which I will choose,
the craftsman use, to write the words
upon the stone. The alphabet's his missal.

Weathering in a wild place, far from here,
read by the spider's glancing feet, your life,
your death, carved into stone, will be
mossed over, brushed by rough grasses,
splashed by waters from the rush-fringed lake
where, one sweltering afternoon, arriving late,
I stood and watched you, your sleeves
rolled high, rowing your boat, already far out.

Grandpa Joe

My Grandpa Joe
was a rag and bone man.
He'd a rickety cart
which he dragged behind him.
It rattled and clattered
down the back streets of Christchurch.
And at every corner,
he'd stop and he'd holler
Hello, hello! Any old iron?

Nobody knew
where Grandpa had come from.
He didn't give the place a name,
he just called it 'Home'.
When the accident happened
after two months in this country,
left without a father,
he wished he never had come here
and Great-Grandma
couldn't stop crying.

Grandpa kept a horse
but it was a lame one
and a dear old donkey
we all called 'High Jinks'.

And three mangy dogs
that always were barking.
In the end Grandpa died—
of hydatids, I think.

Looking for a Grandmother

Each time I focus on my grandmother,
she coughs a little, shifts position,
and stepping back, is lost in the pool
of shadows beneath the overhanging cedar tree.
She's there but I can't find her.

'I'm Swedish', she whispers
as she looks in the mirror,
carefully adjusting the veil
on her hat. Or Norwegian.
Last week she was Danish.
No, born in London.
Or somewhere like that.

'Your grandmother's
coming through town today', said my mother.
'*And* it's your birthday, *and* you can ride
your new bike to school. On the way there,
we can stop at the crossing, wave
to your granny who'll be on a train that's
passing this way.'

The last time I saw her
was on the street where she lived.
I was twelve then and cycling
to school. She seemed quite alone
and she leaned on a gate. I cycled
on as if I'd not seen her,
pretending that I was afraid
to be late.

This Place

Great God! This is an awful place!
Yet there is nothing for it but to stick it to the end.
The snow at last falls softer, slower on our shoulders.
We all know death cannot be long now.

Their memorials rise on pleasant ground,
those men whom all the world names as heroes.
Death and destruction not far behind them,
they cast their shadow on well-trimmed lawns.

They cast their shadow on well-trimmed lawns
death and destruction not far behind them,
those men whom all the world names as heroes.
Their memorials rise on pleasant ground.

We all know death cannot be long now.
The snow at last falls softer, slower on our shoulders.
Yet there is nothing for it but to stick it to the end.
Great God! This is an awful place!

The Last Day It Snowed

Snow. There was only snow.
North or South, it scarcely made a difference
and the present was a time that happened long ago.
Every day had lost its definition. Words escaped us,
had slipped from our vocabulary.
Whiteout obliterates all horizons.

When speaking became too much,
we recognised the failure in ourselves
but held back, it being too great a truth
to be confessed
for now there was no direction.
There was only snow.
We continued the daily count of steps.

Back to the Room

Up early, my footfall's soft upon the stair.
I look through the half-opened door,
the scene's the same.
His back to the room, he's holding a newspaper
taut against the fireplace,
trying to coax flames from the dying embers.
No flames come.
I cannot remember a single conversation with my father.

Child and the Star Book

Blackboard and chalk. Last lesson over,
the teacher called the child back, gave her
a book about the stars. A gift, he said,
because she asked so many questions.
The next day, his boat would be leaving.

His people knew many ways
to find an island. By watching
for change in the patterns of waves,
by following the flight-path of cuckoos or plovers,
by scanning the night sky for familiar stars.

Black feathers fluttered from spars.
Ancestral chants held firm to the rhythm of oars.
Flaxen sails billowed with wind and with song.
'Float lightly, float lightly, my sailing-canoe.
Here is your husband, Ariki-tapu, the Sea.'

She feels the wind tug at her hair,
sea-splash on her cheek. The evening sky
explodes—is brilliant with the fireworks of stars.

In daytime and dreamtime, the child
walks down to the shore of Pegasus Bay
where, treading air, a white horse with wings
has been seen, ready to fly.

She takes out her book
and she reads it again.

There are many ways to find an island.

Uncle from Rome

Every hostess in Naples
tries to find one, don't they?
An Uncle from Rome? Someone who's
hired out from an agency, a sharp dresser,
smart talker who is charming to guests,
adds glamour, excitement. Adds tone?

O, cara mia, have you not met
my dear Uncle Giuseppe from Rome?
He's come straight from a conference
of world leaders in Geneva. He's only just back.

Uncles arrive at the station
on the mornings of marriages,
but usually the tension
is heightened by rumours of doubt.
Will he make it in time?
The Rome meeting's extended?
Yet here's the train now!
And Uncle is always the first to step out.

Although fakers, they always
know what it takes to impress.
Uncle usually is the first to leave parties,
bows low as he offers his host his apologies
mentions a final performance he's attending

'Rigoletto' that evening—a long return journey to Rome.
He catches the train back to his village.
In ten minutes he's home.

Speaking of Mountains:
The Land of the Long White Cloud

Nobody remembered the way
to the mountains, and the track
to the sea was brambled over.
There was no way out.
We were people of the plains;
we had arrived at our grandfathers'
destination and must be glad.

An interruption in a cloudless sky,
the mountains rose above the red roofs
of our town but were as distant
and untouchable as any rainbow
viewed above the stunted trees
at the end of the garden.
We never spoke of the mountains.
They were the hour's journey
there was no need to take. They
were the silences in our conversation.

But if at last the light changed
and we found the way out,
abandoning our father's paradise,
there could be no return except
by crossing the sea and the mountains,
now impossible to ignore
in their vast, blue, folded silences.

Back in a small town on the plains,
sheep graze where our house once was,
the wooden church no longer stands.
The schoolroom gone,
and you no longer there.
I do not recognise anything.
Only the mountains.

Woodsmoke

And all that remained
at the end of our days
were the twists of pale woodsmoke
drifting up from the bonfire
at the end of what had once been our garden.

Smoke looped around empty doorways,
connected with the purple teardrops of
wisteria, then
paused for a moment, dissolved for a moment,
stopped short in mid air, remembered
the blackbird as it sang from the pear tree.

At the Turning

As if, from a distant kitchen,
there's a sound of breaking glass
which is never afterwards explained
but which troubles you forever.
As if you're woken just past midnight
by a familiar voice grown strident,
He's arguing outside your bedroom window,
with a woman whose voice you can't recognise.
We are born, we die, we change.

One winter's night you'd stayed out late,
then stumbled back along the track in darkness.
How quickly what's familiar turns indifferent
when subsumed by dark. For nothing's settled
nothing's known. The old ivied brick wall
you clutch at keeps its secrets, like
final words of an interminable sentence
lose their connection.

But further ahead, there's punctuation
of pure light. A galaxy of glow worms,
those known to Greeks as 'the shining ones'
cluster near the angle of the wall.
Shatterings of fallen stars.
Leavings of light,
transforming the dark.
Interpreters of change.

Moving on Ice

We walked back
through the Great Gate,
as far as the bridge.
A duck swooped from the air,
landed, defeated,
slithering on ice.

It was time to return.
I took her hand.
The child had been quiet
all day.
Her tears fell as softly on snow
as they had done on grass.

We pushed on the gate,
walked up to the house.
Flowers grew through the window
where frost patterns
had, as we left,
been etched on the glass.

Dark Awakenings

Dark awakenings take fresh holdings of the day.
The weight of early light. The rate the heart beats.
Or else withdraws.
Nevermore's the final word the ravens say.

The sky grows restless after evensong. The people pray.
The choir leaves, stands just outside the chapel door.
Dark awakenings take fresh holdings of the day.

No words of mine will prolong the day-lily's stay
for it's not subject to my command but to Nature's law.
Nevermore's the final word the ravens say.

Tomorrow, I'll take the track back to the bay.
A ship is leaving, bound for my native shore.
Dark awakenings take fresh holdings of the day.

Finale. The last Act is over. No more words to say.
The world's no longer a place I will explore.
Nevermore's the final word the ravens say.

Yet a thousand dark awakenings count as nothing,
against the shimmerings of a silvery day I lived before
dark awakenings took fresh holdings of the day.
And I heard the final word the ravens say.

Entering the Frame

But still I'm trying to enter each day
by stepping inside the battered frame
of the painting which hung long ago
on my grandmother's bedroom wall.
There pink and blue fairies lurked
in caves, lingered at entrances to grottos
where no late afternoon shadows ever fell.

Wanting this day to hold for me
something mysterious, dangerous,
wonderful. I will learn to fly.
Already, there on the rock ledge,
I can see the pink phantoms,
up early, catching the sun's
first rays, stretching shimmering
wings, shivering in the cold light
before lifting off, silent as moths.
Ready for a day's fairying.

Sleeping in a Strange Room

after PROUST

With its ice-blue walls, this room's
a crevasse—big as the dome
of St Paul's—into which I have fallen.
My torchlight scrapes along the dark,
finding a future in which I've no part.

Or, slung between rhythms of the womb
and the candlelit requiem round the tomb
I lie smothered in lilies; frail forms surround
me as I wait for the morning's swinging bell
that will call me to heaven or hell.

Survivor of the mysteries of night,
straining towards the high window's light,
this lily's all twisted stalk and listlessness.
The bell tolls *death-in-life,* the bell tolls *life-in-death.*
Capture the earth's last perfumed breath.

Firstborn

November, visiting Vermont. We trudged
through the snow while you skied over
and were the first to reach our cabin,
reading Latin verse by the fireside
while we silently sipped our cocoa.

London. An evening of Beethoven.
We stayed to the end, joining in the applause,
but you left noisily at half-time, smirking
with the wisdom of the boy who has seen
that the Emperor has no clothes.

Always the first to leave, one spring day
you vanished, leaving no footprints
that we could follow. Now we're free
to laugh, to dance, to sing.
We are the firstborn.

Word Attack

I remember the conversation
clinging to the sickly breath
of September sunlight
invading the airless room.

Words goose-stepped
over the kitchen table,
advanced up walls,
hung on the ceiling,

delayed their attack
until dark, and then,
an army of monstrous spiders
fell on hunched shoulders,
two bowed heads.

Bringing Back Birdman

Behind the iridescence
of his paua shell eyes,
beneath the moko carved
and painted on his chin,
skeletons of tiny birds
shift and settle in his head,
bring bone-rattle
    to the skies.

We watch over him. Men
file across wet sands, drop
beside the kite a heap
of clattering cockle shells,
tie them to his tail as weights.
Oh Tāwhirimātea!
god who moves the winds,
    may they rise!

The god replies. Gusts ruffle
green kākā feathers sewn
to Birdman's barkcloth chest.
He breathes. Trembles. Ready
to head skywards as we chant:
Ascend on high, Tāwhaki!
Go to the first, then
to the second heaven!

What does it matter
if Birdman's music
is only bone-song,
shell-chatter? Look up!
    he flies!

Ravenous

How far did you become a bird
when they dressed you in feathers?
when, with beak-bruised fingers,
they drew down on to your shoulders
the great bird mask?

Unhallowed boy, part-raven,
hurled at the heavens, skewered
to the sun's slipstream,
whose was the hunger
that set you off on flight?

As I look along the sky's dark corridor
on starless evenings, your ashy imprint
lurks, spread-eagled against glass.
The crash and burn of bird
become a cruciform of dust.

Kites were sometimes used for divination. Only the tribal leaders knew the spells necessary to make kites fly. Birdman kites have wings, a more or less human-shaped body, and a head with a hawk or kākā (parrot) feathers for hair, shells for eyes and a moko (tattoo) on his chin.

Mollusc Child

Small, pale, thumb-shaped,
you perched at the end
of my bed last night, smiling,
(I wanted to keep you smiling)
like one of your childhood
drawings, those I keep,
those that are lost.

Shape-shifter, mollusc
escaped from your shell
while my eyes were closed,
Are you still my child?
And where is your own?

Hold your child tightly.
Someone will teach her
to fear change. She knows
you would die for her,
knows too that a time
will come when that
will not be enough.

Keep smiling, my mollusc child.

The Fallen

Our willow had seen too much sky,
endured a plethora of broad-canvassed
fenland sunsets. Throughout
the storm of a summer night
its branches groaned, and
in the morning the willow lay
huge, stricken, aslant the lawn,
trails of unkempt green hair
weeping into earth. It was
not a planned death.

Gingerly, the old cat stepped
along the trunk, testing it for treeness,
revising theories of permanence
and destination. For the fallen
and those they leave behind,
old age is no preparation.

Hanging on the Hickory

I thought I was in an empty room.
But he was there.
With his lariats, he'd hunkered down
behind the open door.
His sudden move. A hurl of ropes
which falling, overlapped
the door. As they swung back,

I heard the dolls' heads crack, the scrape
of tiny fingernails on wood.
Both frail cloth necks
were tightly noosed:
my skipping rope, his dressing gown cord.

He dipped the ropes, but still
I couldn't pull them down.
My empty hands clawed at the door;
he'd jerked the ropes back up again.

A final try, my very last chance,
becomes my brother's victory.
The name he gave to the game he played
was Hanging on the Hickory.

Acorn People

The dolls we had as presents
seldom settled in our house.
My sister's Shirley Temple doll,
flown in from Hollywood, smiled
bravely for some photo shoots
and one day when we looked
for her, we found she'd gone.

The ugly, stern-faced doll
called Ermintrude, left over
at the jumble sale, seemed
not to like her name, stared
crossly from beneath
her mustard-coloured velvet hat.
At the next sale in the village,
without a word to any of us,
Ermintrude went back.

We filled the dolls' house
that my father built
with matchbox furniture
we'd made ourselves,
bent safety pins for drawer handles,
old clothes cut up for sheets.
The beds stayed mostly empty,
though we'd invented families
of acorn people who
should have been the perfect size.

They didn't stay long, for when
the dolls' house was the place
to store old newspapers, floor-to-ceiling,
to stuff in dusters, shifted
to the darkest corner of the washhouse
where spiders dangled overhead,
the acorn people left.

A Shadow of Myself

This morning you caught me
trying to pick up a shadow
from the breakfast table,
I, not quite knowing
what shade of self
it was that, lying there,
eclipsed the sun.

It was as if from within
a neighbouring house
which each day we'd passed as children,
but from which we had never seen
a leaving or an entering,
one day we heard music, voices.
I walked up the steps, turned the key.
The door opened.
I went in.